AF236419

*Faces of the day*
*Poems, thought texts and lyrics*

Sebastian Moritz

2022

# Faces of the day

Poems, thought texts and lyrics

Author
Sebastian Moritz

Year 2022

Imprint © 2022 Sebastian Moritz; Haakestraße 48, 21075 Hamburg;
Sebastian_Moritz.Autor@web.de

Production and publishing: BoD - Books on Demand, Norderstedt

ISBN: 9783755795704

"Poetry, the skill of the thinker who knows no limits in his word formation."

—Sebastian Moritz

# Contents

# Poetry

# PREFACE

*The poetry and the song are a part of me,*
*so love me one,*
*weigh me a part of you,*
*without whom I do not want to have*
*been.*

—Sebastian Moritz

*D*ays are not infinite. The day itself and the days that we live in life. But with the finiteness of a day, of life, with all its natural and sometimes unnatural rhythms, it is up to the person himself to cancel what seems impossible at the given boundaries and in between. In our imagination, in the strength from which as humans we can draw hope, in everyday things, small and large miracles of life and its nature that shape us. Who we are as people and who we want to be.

These texts should make a contribution to recognizing the impossible by developing one's own ideas, using one's senses and feelings as a human being to overcome the boundaries that sometimes seem too big. Indeed, it is these limits that help to determine the feeling of life, just as our daily actions are shaped by what we recognize and want to achieve in our life.

No life will go by without the feelings that make us human, because feelings are real, just like our perception as humans, this day and on the days of our lives. Giving this one expression is a fundamental theme of the texts and the idea behind writing this book.

*It is precisely these feelings that are greater than anything that we cannot promise ourselves from a life as human beings alone, at least if we cannot share and live it together.*

# THOUGHT RICHES

## 1
### Good things that wouldn't be

Now only the suffering was so great
Or I didn't know what it was
so as not to postpone fate,
Time has passed by on the line
Thrive without spoilage

It was like that
incorporated in the sand
If shards of glass fell on stones,
It turned out much bigger than
time did not expect
Good things that wouldn't be.

## 2
### Imagined realms

I wasn't from the wind of a hurry
      pulled along over land to sea,
Sailing in imaginary realms
      The unimpressive Rain that did
        not fall from the rain drip,
Shuddering rain that would never be

A sheet flowing without a direction
      fell about in an unsteady tumble,
So heavy from the wet
      Wasn't it just a good memory of
        absolutly being free,
A place where nobody would be.

### 3
### Hardly any light in sight

Light is dense
   in the shining intertwined around me
Seas of shadow covered by clouds of mist
   their desolate glances turned gray in the
      shimmer

I did not see a single cloud in the dark light
   a crack-like passage of dimmed light flurries
      so heavily
The tall trunks of the thick trunks
   Deeply beaten in the bridle of darkness
they have fallen into disrepair

Full of shadows in the light of a tall tree
   Intertwined in a labyrinth of forks in
      the light-flooded gray
Didn't want to live in the shadowy light
   don't believe my own eyes.

4
Palace of thought

I built you a castle so huge
So far in my mind
And so rich in thought,
The incredible place where there
is happiness in the world
It would not last forever on earth

With deep and wide trenches
And with high walls and towers
Towered further into the sky,
To keep the most precious thing
on earth
Just having a single thought

And I don't just keep thinking only
about you
Senses and emotions that were
carved deep in stone
I thought just lucky for you,
A pretty palace adorned with
waving flags
all of my thoughts that were surrounded
by you.

## 5
### Soul lakes in black

In the blackness of the soul's lakes
Immersed in the black
I washed off glittering pearls

Carefully lowered from intermediate
worlds
Falling into an infinite sleep
They lay unnoticed at the bottom of
the soul
Found treasures of memory

Unmolested a thought from all time
Soul grounds in black lakes
Shine full of passion.

6
Bedded dreams

I took it from you
    heavy on your shoulders,
the sky trucks were hanging down:
    Fallen out of the clouds
appeared so easy,
    They came from high above:
Carried a child in the evening breeze
    Sufferings that call me they strived for
        life and flew me around:
Climbed from heaven high
    Buried deep under all earth,
All of my dreams that lay on the ground.

# PASSAGE INTO ANOTHER WORLD

7

Passage into another world


In the dark and deserted back room
          A secret door was set between
                    wooden calluses
          if there was a secret, a incomprehensible
                    gate of impenetrability,
          Its narrow and forgotten lines
                    split in the shadow
          Open to the immortal
                    it wasn't for a brief moment
                    that stayed

          Seen what no one did not know
                    Cursed into the great door, Gates
                    of Time
          I did not fear the unknown,
                    An invisible border was painted
                    with white paint on the bare
                    wall of the room
          A shimmer of light reflected in the
                    pale gray
                    the passage into another world.

## 8
*Sadness within me alone*

My grief is there alone
　　　where I didn't see anyone
　　　　myself,
Out of sheer loneliness
　　abandoned in the dark

Shadows in eternal light
　　I was already grieving,
Where had I not been
　　where I myself could not
　　　have trusted my face

A place was hidden in me
　　I live there forever,
So many others mourned where
　　　I hadn't been myself
　　when no one can mourn
　　alone.

9
*Lights of my world*

I curled up eagerly, the lights of the sky
They were clenched into a fist in
my plaintive hand,
A portrait of my heavenly world
Drawn with the light and dark
colors,
Glossy and matt, in all imaginable
colors
On a piece of flaky paper

It glittered and it seemed to be my
world
From the dark, a light that shines
so bright
It was so loose and so brittle for me
My world,
And shine out of my skin
That it falls apart in her.

10
*Rain of stars*

Trickling so soothes a slight tickling
    From snow-white clouds in the distance
        from high above
Come from a completely different world,
    The many many small, finest lights
Carefully laid down in bed on earth

Stirred gently in the dubious glow of many
        tiny clouds
    Covered up in a deep slumber
The many small lights shine in a golden-
        yellow feather shoe,
    Come on earth, well protected in life
Surrounded her with a sweet dream of a
        completely different world.

# FOUR SEASONS PASS

## 11
### Four seasons pass


Four seasons passed
> I never expected spring, and summer
> again

The summer sun meadows in spring
> they thrived
> > so wonderful, so beautiful they
> > lose

So the time will have come again for
> them to go down in the glow
> of the summer sun

In the autumn you could see their
> leaves slowly fall
> > Its colors, lost in gray-blue tones,
> > crossed the land in the lush
> > green

In the white winter it will be the
> same for the very last time
> so beautiful they lose

Stand still, and time stood still in
> four seasons.

## 12
### Heather

Heather, you purple green
    You bloomed from autumn to summer
Show your colorful ones
    Meaded immortal bloom times

Pink, red and white green
    Winter time and spring days
Tell me what color you wear
    your bloom will never fade away.

13
All the sky lights

The last star, turns off its little light
    Eternal appearance, not eternal
    seemed
So he will have been a little light,
    At some point the time comes when
    every star turns off its little
    light,
Long times, in the sky shine
    My eternal glow, can't seem forever
    For you and for me
All the lights of the sky, they shine
    so bright,
    Long times, in the sky shine
For you, for me, for all time
    All the little lights, so bright in
    the starry sky
Shine into the world.

## 14
### The world full bloomed.


The world amazes
　　Wilt the world to be

The world in full bloom,
　　The leaf fell

A world full of bloom
　　To be blossoms in the world.

15
All bright colors


Uniquely colorful flower
    What did you tell me?
All colors, oh wonder!
    All the colors faded in wilt,

Didn't understand a word
    You revolt in the light,
Your colors are so colorful, oh I
        was amazed!
    Colorful in the silver light,

Wore bright colors
    Your endlessly beautiful word
        sheet will never fade,
Just tell me one word from you
    I can see all the colored lights.

# MOONS THAT RISE AND SUNS THAT SET

## 16
### Moons that rise and suns that set

The pale moon shines bright
    In the bright morning sky,
Divorced from the endlessness of time

And the rising sun gave him its shimmer
    they would move into the invisible,
And in the morning new lights came on

So his maturity would forever be his
    Every new day would have happened
        just like this,
Shining sky in the ascended opening

A world in the glimmer of hope
    Where no one has looked,
Moons that rise and suns that set.

## 17
### The sun and the sea

When the sun and the sea met
      In the evening and the
            morning,
      Ascended and sunk
            Beyond the horizon was
                  infinity

      An apparent touch
            Noticeably gentle and very
                  supple as it would not
                  have been,
      It had passed so quickly
            A feeling of draining.

### 18
#### Dancing between the days

Four moons had already passed
    I didn't see the third of them coming

So there were already three that hadn't quite
        passed
    Hadn't seen the last of them coming

So I didn't forget what was in between
    I will probably not see the sun, its rays
    again,

Only one of them, hadn't it been too much
        of a good thing,
    One more, I'll never see it again

The sunshine is split,
    it danced between the days that never
    seemed quite gone

But this one more, I forgot it again,
    Can I see the sunlight only once again?

# INVISIBLE BARRIER

19
Love bed


And when I've been poor
    Empty in my faded skin
I didn't think of sleep and rest that I couldn't
        find in myself
    I was nothing without you
All the dreams that didn't go away
    A dream that I didn't dream

The coolness and coldness that I didn't miss
    Cover my frozen shell gently with your
        warming hands
So that I can fall from the sky
    Covered in your love
Surrender me in my dreams in which I may
    have been with you.

20
*Invisible barrier*


Whenever I stand at your barrier
  Invisible and yet insurmountable,
Alone in the goodness and purity of your
      great heart
  I don't like to see what is in front of me

I saw you and I didn't stop
  One step and another towards you, every
      step I took with you,
Once closer it was unreachable
  I saw you and your love, so pure.

21
Beauty alone is not

Preserve your beauty
    did not arise from your reputation,
The face is not an spitting image
    How you would have been

As people alone
    unseen the person I was not,
Nice that it was you
    That I've seen the beauty once again.

## 22
### My desire


All becoming
    That's why I was never myself
Wasn't it still mine to myself?
    Your desire and desire to satisfy your
        longings

Faithful not to forgive myself
    With all becoming it was gone
With everything that has been
    My own, so as not to forgive myself.

## 23
### Steadfast love

Maybe it was just once in my dreams
That I protected love with all my might

Openly my vulnerable heart lay there alone
and abandoned
Because I was killed by her

Badly hit without warning
At the same time gentle and merciless

I had broken down in my dreams
Stopped in front of love to love you.

## 24
### A summer night

Didn't I promise you a summer night
   Much more beautiful than the evening
     didn't go by,
And the morning hadn't come
   That made her the new day

Because all time would go by
   In a single summer night,
The evanescence was so beautiful
   If I had spent it with you.

25
Alone, alone


Often my heart only broke two things
    But it was lonely for me
Of two alone,
    One alone
Alone, alone

Often it was just gone
    One of all sorts
For you it wasn't one of many,
    One alone
Alone, alone

For you now it is part of two
    From you to me to one alone
I from you a part to mine
    One alone
Alone, alone

Will love you forever
    From one alone
From mine to yours
    Just to be a part of you
Alone, alone.

### 26
### By your side

Jumped up,
    To be happy by your side

Turned to pleasure
    Screws turn,
Jumped up by your side

Sea width
    Prepare the way for you,
Don't leave your side while jumping through

Width by width,
    To be happy by your side.

# NOBODY'S NIGHT

27
Nobody's night

Don't punish me, because I am freed from
        all my senses,
    Whether day moon or twilight of all the
        good gods
Surrounded by all spirits,
    Often no, had it not been admitted
Please, don't call me for mercy

Freed from all life
    It would never have been there for me,
Forgotten was the time
    That would never have come after it,
Truth not promised
    Didn't they confess me a reward?

Countless things had already passed,
    Fearful the child spoke out of his cheeky
        mouth
Freedom I saw it clearly in the starry sky
    light at nobody's night,
    That no one believes has seen
A child that child cannot be.

## 28
### What the right is not

Everything that is bad is not all right
But I don't like the bad
What is bad is what the right
is not

So I don't ask to ask
So I don't doubt it
And I didn't doubt to ask what
the right is not.

29
Shadow blossoms star telling

There where in the vastness and unfathomable
    darkness a little shimmer waited in
    the thicket of shine
A whisper secretly drifted clammy across
    the vast ground
Lurking in the foggy green twilight
    The patch of shadow that remained in
    impregnable darkness

Didn't seek eternal rest in the silence of unseen
    nights
    The light that played in the moon and the
    stars read that wise men lay hiding
    places
Bedded in the head of high crowns
    Its shadow pervaded by a bluish glow of
    dense purity

Night light where otherwise only a shadow
field is waiting indispensable
For a long time they had been waiting in
the opaque niece in front of expectant
lights
Starlight illuminates and all density density
discomfort
Forests stretches across unimagined fields
and lush green meadows full of fruit,
buds and shadowy blossoms, star tales.

30
Nobody's time


It didn't help anyone
    With timelessness,
and the time that was not infinite
    With everything that was not forgotten

I'm not nobody
    At no one's time,
I am nobody's love and nobody's joy
    With everything that helped nobody

It wasn't me
    I wasn't,
What time, joy and love was not
    What never was, what nobody was not.

# THE WHITE RIVER

31
The white river


Risen to white strands
    From giant shoulders mountains,
Slid on elven wings
    Carefully carried to the valley

Fine branches that twine for ways
    In all your arms embracing your wings,
Covered in your shallow pool
    They lay on white beds

Encompassed the farthest lands
    On paths that were leveled,
In rich soils and sinks
    They ensnared all lifelines

The white threads flow
    Fertility from your jump,
From elves feathers white hair
    Rivers that protrude into the great seas.

32
*Rest in the silence*

Rest in the silence
    Deep asleep,
Width below me

Stone and rubble
    No burden swept up,
Far below me

Expanse in the silence
    Where the water lives,
My soul floated up

Depth far below me
    Never hollowed out in hides and bellies,
I lived where the water lives

A storm in the distance
    Live on a drive,
Get it for me

Swaying and swaying
    Showed up,
Lived up with you

There was no emptiness
    My soul lived,
Through and through

Drive up
    My life,
What the sea did not have in me.

33
Got distance in my head

Got distance in my head
    My longing, it lies far behind the way
The distance that was still ahead of me
        There, behind this raised wall of sand
            and stone,
the many houses, thick walls,
    the big cities, a country far beyond the
        wide horizon,
Traveled far across seas and mountains,
    where far away would not be, the distance


For long long days, unreached
    Places that are home to me
They were in my head
    My longings so far away,
And was I somewhere else, there
    Where home wouldn't be for me,
So it stays in my head
    Home so far away from me.

34
A pearl of the world


A large gate stood completely open
　　So it led me to the world,
Everyone's friend
　　Friends shared all over the world

On water, its routes
　　Grounds of his ways on earth,
Smooth well on high waves
　　Filed a pearl of worlds

From the heart's joyous sounds
　　And home banks of its ports,
Rough cut in the sand
　　Nothing but his honesty

It leads me to every home
　　Left no one on worlds alone,
The hanseatic city remains a honest world
　　　　to every friend
　　A place where the world unites.

# MILLING MILLS

35
The wet stone


Keel hold up
    It hit the plank in high gear

Broken from the ridge by the waves
    It fell on the wet stone

The ship flees from the side skeleton
    Trims the mast in the harsh wind

Sails stiff bent in the wind
    Flown for a long time

Hold mast and break the sheet
    Broken before the wet stone.

### 36
#### Soft iron heart

Forge iron
   It glowed white brightly

Hammer his forge
   Courageous weight,

Soft melt
   Brittle broke quickly,

Forge iron heart
   It's not breaking.

37
Milling mills


Turns laboriously in the mild wind
 A gear train so heavy
that ground it so finely
 Grind mills on a large grater

Grist and chaff
 Wheat gold in the sleeve dress
refresh the body with lively mouths
 The barley should have full mouths.

# ALL LIGHTS OUT

## 38
### All lights out


All lights out, everything goes quiet, the
      lonely man plays a little song on the
      piano,

A song that speaks of the simple life and its
      frivolity,
      In endless lines that only the pure spirit
      and the freest of all souls can understand


For every person, free of all senses, a person
      who can hear his little song just once
      more,
      So often and so long until the last little
      light goes out, so often and so long
      until the last of all people can understand


The lines of life, with all its things, with all
      trimmings and trallala, with trumpets
      from the stars and everything that
      goes with it,
      A song that no one can hear again

*So it is once again quiet, the silence of the
    night, silence in the many houses and
    the deserted streets, even if the last
    of all days was not yet over,
Here and now, the lines of life, for a long
    time as they had never been heard
    before.*

### 39
#### Old worry songs

First it was the burden, so quietly
    the old man wears them carelessly
Around with you on all paths of life
    Carefree, as if the last few days were far
        from over

Did he take it much easy, lie on his hunched
        shoulders
    Heavy trucks that weigh to the ground
And weighed the burden so heavy
    Away in the day that's still a long way
        from being

Did they fall suddenly, mute and barren
    His heavy limbs moaned loudly
With the sounds of worry pressed him down
    Heavy vices, old sorrows sang old songs.

## 40
### The thick tuba


The thick tuba
   Blown perky mouths
In wide tubes and stalks,
   Pressed into winding caves
Fan dull and heavy

Didn't you hear the ringing
   A peace in the depths
I feel the hall,
   At the bottom my depth
I blew deep into it.

41
Violins his singing

Violins his singing
    Singed very softly,
I cut a tone
    Melodies rang out,
of life they sang

Stroke in the thread they walked
    Sounds drawn from my hand,
You pull on sides very tense
    Songs that sounded,
who played about life.

# NOTEPADS

## 42
### Without words

Talking without a voice
    Words, sentences in innumerable ointment
        tones,
They had fallen from unspeakable heights
        down deep inside me
    Sunk deep in my body,
Choked it because I didn't say a word to you

They pushed out of me eagerly
    Things not said without a voice,
As they would never have been said
    Didn't they promise me another world,
Once they spoke of you without a word

My hands closed in front of my mouth
    Searched desperately in endless words
        and sentences,
Didn't hear the voice in my chest
    I was denied a world without a voice,
I didn't speak a word to you.

43
Notepads


I collect writing pads
    Without any content,
For the unforgotten
    and for the imperishable,
So that it would never be forgotten
    and there is no forgetting gone

Nothingness that did not translate itself to
        me like nothing that could be
    That I didn't make it up for myself,
Thought that I'm already losing it
    contrary to expectations and unattainable
        things next to me,
The writing on endless page ends
    on paper full of emptiness.

44
*Pen stroke*

Pen stroke by a hair's width,
    brush's width in the line
drawn by a hair, missed stripe,
    line brush
drawn around the edge on one side.

# GRAY WORLD

45
Gray world


It was an elephant alone
     Black among many others,
Didn't he want to be alone

There came a man
     Jumped up to ride,
Blue should be his color

The world in the gray
     Went crazy around them,
Didn't want to be in colors.

## 46
### Unforgettable figures

The seas cease to flow
    how once the still water fed all the depths
        and hollows of the earth's ground
        anew with a flow of life,

Time of its origin does not forget it, and its
        filth it does not pass,
    as he once washed it completely clean
        and clear of all the scum from the
        earth's ground,

The nature, which gave it its most diverse
        forms, the purity as it was not, which
        has never been given again from ever
        new life,
    before the new life that has never given
        up and spoils everything that has
        never been lived through before,

All innovations, such as the poison that has
        lived through everything before and
        has been corrupted forever,
    which has never happened again since
        the beginning of time.

47
The World around me


Pull me around the world
    around once more,
And tell me
    That this world wasn't eventual

Did I have been dream of unreached gifts
    The world view of immortal nature,
Not alone as it would not be
    so as not to have failed

Didn't see things that weren't
    So tell me,
And I didn't say a word to you
    I don't dream without revolving around
        myself.

## 48
### A thousand new tears


Decay to the finest dust
    Ashes that fell from the sky like snowflakes

From gray it had sunk into black
    Thousands of new tears and the mouths
        that were hungry now
A thousand new tears
    It was the time of horror and fear that
        had now begun

Completely dilapidated from thousands of
        parts, melted away in weakness
    The shine of the whole was now completely
        forgotten, because it would have been
        whole
All the things that were never there

Ashes to dust and seas of sulfur
    It wasn't hurt who hadn't been a wicked
        man
So it had passed, the peace that life would
        have been.

49
Heart burns like fire

It ignites quickly
    Heart burns like fire,
Warmth refreshes my soul
    Embers come from far below

Ashes burned
    A flame from an open hand,
Flaming happiness in the wind blows
    Don't dust go away

Heat is seething from my soul
    Sea of flames blown away,
Fire comes from the heart
    Happiness taken by hand

Crackling hissing
    Sparks don't burn up,
Ashes turned to dust
    Fire is coming from my heart.

# HEAVENLY CAVE SOUNDS

## 50
### Heavenly cave sounds

Up and down on sounding ladders
  A shining bell and the eaves a blessing
Sounds fly through the air

In wide arches sides that swing
  In wide arches of the pages they sing
In the deep waves and high sails echoed

As a mirror a bright shine in all directions
      of the sky
  And in the light they played down all
      the beautiful tunes
Where a human could hear it

Shooting stars full of splendor all songs and
      chants
  A tower built up to the sounds of heavenly
      caves
The sound that life hears.

## 51
### In far distance

I climbed the distant hills and fields, the
    peaks of the mountains
  Where under all the tricky steps that I
    climbed,
My doubts were on the ground

On my way forward
  I left them there, lost in the distance,
With every step that my feet carried me on

And still I will look further
  After all the remote reasons,
From where they could be seen

Far away, in all highs and lows
  And my day will bring me further,
A little further forward

To unreached heights and expanses, where
    they were still the basis
  Every step I took,
To find my freedom in the world.

52
Shine of the world

A shine in the world
   Didn't he sound
In the hall of the world
   full of sunshine,
The splendor of the world
   Doesn't he seem
into me, forever

I didn't sing so fine
   A song of bliss
So it echoed in the world
   lovely voices,
Voices so pure
   Life forever times
abundant its ages.

## 53
### The silence of the music

Out of the silence alone,
   nobody heard it
was it music,
   emerged from nowhere

It was heard alone,
   no sound in the world
drawn unheard of,
   dissolved in thin air

Where there was no silence,
   Strings, plucks and in caves
sung and play with touch,
   The silence of the music.

# FACES OF THE DAY

54
Faces of the day


Day, you don't see the sun
    Too long already passed, what seemed to
        be underneath,
Behind the curtain, there it was hidden
    The inimitable figure, the night game:
Day, you don't see the sun
    All around, all the bright colors,
In blue and yellow faces, folded
    In black and dark tail, ages
Your robe, in colors the faded
    The night, stripped by your light,
Didn't you see the sun?
    On days when the sun shines so brightly,
        and recently does not shine.

## 55
### I don't dream a lot

It was just a dream to me
   I dreamed of a lot,
What I don't have
   And what I don't know,
A dream of so many

So equipped my fantasies
   Worlds in my dreams,
What I want
   And am willing to know,
It remained a dream to me.

56
Remaining

I picked up the little lights again,
    that once fell too low
so small and inconspicuous seemed to me,
    drifting in the abyss
on black floors, lay down again

A desolate existence,
    revealed the size to me
my boundless world,
    with giant hands and long arms I reached
        for them
out of indifference it had remained for all
        the time.

## 57
### Starry sky beds

Starry sky beds in the blaze of lights at time
   Tail of the blackened nights,
covered by rays

A cradle of light bills
   Starlight blackness,
Placed in the bowl of the night

A twinkling star in the sky bed
   The nights at times,
Near and so far away that they realize.

# LIFE

## 58
## Life

Finally, they are not
   All days passed,
A new life,
   Of the heart:
To mean the times,
   Don't forget to beat it,
So it beats with all imaginable force,
   That it is life.

## 59
### My ghost


My skin
    Has she gotten so old
From the long wait,
    But my mind
Isn't it?

In an origin
    Where it has already been
Not like my life,
    But I'm old
Like he's never been.

60
People just like us

How wonderful, can it be time to wait
If only new life arises
For love us, the truth has remained
People just like us:
People only, the truth remains
If we only have one life left
Longed for out of our love.

## 61
### Past and oblivion

If I didn't know
   How old life really is,
I wouldn't be afraid to live for it

That it is not perishable
   Past and oblivion,
Not life, that it is not life for me.

## 62
### Look into the distance

When you look into the distance
    After a moment, you were looking for
        that,
Along the river where stone broke it on opposite
        banks
    From the bridge that was still ahead of
        me

And the water splashed to itself
    After all the unimagined times that were
        still missing,
For a while I let the direction of my presence
    At the bottom, he was
sunk in the old valley.

# THE KNOWLEDGE OF
# THE QUIET

## 63
### The knowledge of the quiet


Silent lines,
    Silent way

Speak softly,
    When you speak,
Speak of the wise men

The knowledge of old days,
    The old sage,
That everything new keeps me

Speak quietly,
    Be wise.

## 64
### I foresee

I foresee,
    Where is the light?
Without that I have no beginning and no
        end of my time,
    the intermediate world that is actually
        your life
Can't have seen for a long time:
    The sky seems so endlessly free
Without my dreams and the light of life as
        it has not already passed,
    Can't have seen in a while.

65
White doves

I know that the doves were white
    Yes, they were,
Yesterday, tomorrow
    And every other day,
Oh, how the time passed

The white doves
    There they fly,
They didn't come back
    That I don't see them after all,
White doves, with white plumage.

66
To all glory


Fall, fall deep down
    or I get up.
With thousands of leaves, flowers, buds
    Sink in my arms,
Or do I rise, my head
    to unreached heights
wherever you looked.
    Life in all my glory.

# SANDS OF TIME

67
Sands of time


I sank endlessly deep
   In the sands of time

One grain for every second
   Every moment that has been,
She counted against me

A helpless reach into nowhere
   I flowed in the river,
No more stopping that remains

Not stopped at any reason
   Where there was still time.

## 68
### The time how it passed

Sometimes I took,
    Aged a lot,
A little time out,
    Older than I actually am
To get there,
    And I don't have a day
To live and to die,
    To this finiteness
To whom it was concerned,
    And showed me my own end
Finally to understand.

69
Train of time


I like to travel,
	From the origin of my time
Where mine wasn't,
	Until the day that life is over

On rails,
	Chattering wheels of the past
Did they meet in infinity,
	And my train derailed from time.

## 70
### New Years

With a little wink
    I say goodbye to the days,
For new years, new luck
    Moments that I kept for myself,
All my days never gone
    To a new year, new luck,
So they stood there in the stars.

# HEAVEN'S BLESSING

71
Heaven's blessing


The sun put me at peace
    Little birds sang a song of happiness
Heaven praised my blessing
    To go all the way to the stars

Got out of the open window
    To float on shallow clouds
Life will be easier forever
    To fly up on angel wings.

72
I listen to sing

I listened from the window of the big door
    And I hear a bright voice
A bright voice that was heard even when I
       didn't sing myself,
    The silence not heard
My soul,
    Forsaken by all ghosts, it seemed lonely
       to me:
What did you say that I don't sing?
    Life is part of me,
A low hum full of voice
    It sounded softly in my fine ear,
Just hear what I'm not singing
    A whisper of life in my fine ear.

73
Chirping hearts


It chirped in my heart
    A little bird must be nesting inside it
A newly-hatched sprout sitting in a nest
    Felt the soothing warmth in his soft feather
        pillow

It chirped a lively spring song
    It was alive and I wanted to fly as high
        and as far as I can
Don't stand still for a second
    If I listen to the sound of life, it will
        never be gone.

# GOLDEN MOON

74

*Golden moon*

*I slept in my sleep*
*Don't sleep now,*
*I was awake at night*

*All night long*
*Do not rest in sleep,*
*I was awake for days*

*Days not slept*
*Don't sleep now,*
*By day and not by night*

*Made the moon gold*
*When I sleep I will rest,*
*By day and not by night.*

75
The chaff goes away


Before dawn
    Bright yellow in the dew of the morning
If the light turns yellow in the white

Wide meadows
    Hollow in the yellow spar
The wheat chaff glimmer in the yellow

Stubble dull
    Clay and earth too gray to the ground

In the sky green
    In the dust the seeds burn up to gray.

76
Shellless thought games

Ease in the foot
   Thoughts came and went,
A silence that lay before the threshold
   Meager feelings and wordless fuss,
Give me up in time
   And the days had passed

My fate quickly seized it
   There was a slight rustling in the fresh
      wind,
In the rush it came through the back door
      unnoticed
   I skipped the days its real time,
Times that had passed
   And the days that haven't been

My oblivion overtakes it
   I caught secret noises unnoticed,
Today joys without a discretion
   A carefree existence for no apparent reason,
     A loose leaf wedged into it
Shellless thought games.

## THE END